Momming and Queening

Presented by
Alesha Shaw

Book Cover Design & Interior Book Design: TamikaINK.com
Editor: Alesha Shaw

Published By: Tamika INK
Library of Congress Cataloging – in- Publication Data has been applied for.

ISBN: 9798525123861

PRINTED IN THE UNITED STATES OF AMERICA.

Table of Contents

Introduction

At the beginning of 2020, I knew something wasn't right. I hadn't felt like myself for months, and I couldn't figure out why. So, I was actually thankful that the pandemic shut us down for a minute. I was able to relax and get my thoughts together. I realize I spent a lot of time giving to everyone else but myself. A lot of my giving went to my girls. Little did I know that was weighing a lot on my mental health. Although I love them both very much, I started to feel like I didn't know what I was doing. On top of that, it is exhausting, it can be hard, and there really is no "go to" manual to it. Sure, you have those experts out there who think they have the answers, but there is nothing like real honest stories about the adventures of motherhood to help get you through the journey.

I have said this once and I will say it over and over. Being a mother is one of the hardest things, I have ever done. Most of the time, let's be honest, ALL of the time, I am winging it, and praying I am not doing any permanent damage. In all that I do, I do it the best of my abilities. Especially if it is something that means a lot to me and will be displayed in some shape of form. Parenting is no different. I am constantly going to God, asking for guidance and wisdom on how to rear these two rugrats of mine. I am also constantly asking for grace for the times that I don't always hold it together. At the end of the day, I do the best that I can as I take on roles of teacher, counselor, chef, housekeeper, mediator, and any other titles that moms have to put on in order to keep a sane household.

When I decided to take on this anthology, my goal was to reach out to moms out there who were just like me. Moms who were rocking out this motherhood thing despite the challenges we face. In today's world, social media sometimes causes us to portray pictures of perfection, but I wanted to share stories of reality. The reality is, we don't always have it together. We don't always have the answers, and we don't always make the best decisions, and that's quite alright. We may not be perfect, but we are definitely queening it.

What is Momming and Queening?

What is momming? Momming is just a slang word I use to described "motherhood." It is what we do every day (refer to the titles mentioned last sentence of the 3rd paragraph). It is a term that I thought was cuter than motherhood and seemed to fit today's language a little bit better. Ok, let's be real, it was just catchy!!

Now, let's get to queening. According to Google, "queening" is behaving in an unpleasantly superior way towards someone. However, that is not how I see or use the word "queening." So that there is no confusion, let's break down what queening is in my eyes and for the sake of this book.

Google also defines a queen as a female ruler of an independent state. It goes on to explain that in the game, Chess, the queen is the most powerful piece on the board. As a mother, a ruler of your independent state (family), you are powerful in your own right. You were honored to be overseers over precious beings. God entrusted you with their lives because He knew what you were capable of doing with them. He knew that you would be able to give them all that they need to make it in this world.

Queening is a frame of mind, a way of carrying yourself. It is walking, confidently in your role as a mother and owning it. Owning all it entails, triumphs and failures. Recognizing that you may not have all the answers and you may not always make the best decisions, but through it all, you rock this thing called Motherhood and nobody can tell you any different. It is wearing that crown, walking that walk, and praying that prayer. Queening is trusting in your power as a mother and raising children of the kingdom. Knowing that through it all God's got your back, and His grace is sufficient, you will not fail. The ladies of this anthology are the epitome of strength and grace. Through the stories that they share, and the work they have done (on themselves and in their families), they are living proof that we are indeed magic. We are rocking this thing! So, sit back and be encouraged by these awesome ladies who are Momming and Queening!

About Alesha Shaw

Alesha Shaw is one of the international best-selling authors of the anthology, "I am More than Enough." She is a proud graduate of HBCU, Prairie View A&M University where she received her BS in Psychology. She also has a MA in Counseling from Webster University. She has several credentials including Licensed Master's Social Worker and Licensed Chemical Dependency Professional. Her aspirations are to use her knowledge and experiences to help women heal old wounds that hinder them from reaching their highest potential self. She has recently taken up blogging and plans to use this as a tool to reach and empower women. She loves all things healing and is big on spirituality. You can find her grooving to a plethora of music genres because music soothes her soul. Raised in El Paso, Texas she is a lover of mountains, sunny days, hot weather, and tacos! She finds joy in seeing others succeed and putting smiles on the faces of people she meets. You can connect with her by following her on Instagram at @thebookofalesha as well as her Facebook page, "The Book of Alesha." Be sure to also visit her website at www.aleshashevon.com.

Momming and Queening: My First Ministry

By Tee Hubbs

What little girl didn't grow up wanting to be a princess? What little girl didn't grow up wanting to be a super-hero? I did! And I don't know about y'all, but at age of seventeen, all of my dreams started coming true! A woman doesn't know her true strength until she has to be strong for another human. I knew I had a superpower when my son was only months old, and I had to watch him in an incubator because he couldn't breathe due to asthma. I stood there and watched him all night and didn't shed a tear. Also, when there were multiple visits to the hospital and the doctor's every other day for breathing treatments, not knowing if my son would ever be able to breathe regularly on his own. I knew that I had moved pass princess status and became a queen when I had to make big girl decisions which meant some major sacrifices. I decided to sacrifice my own future and decided not to go to college or the air force. Instead, I would gracefully wear my crown, fix my posture, and walk into the first ministry that God gave me, Momming and Queening.

Two snaps of the fingers, a neck tilt to the side, and screaming "Yasss hunty!," as I adjust my crown and give myself props after a 12-hour workday, dinner is cooked, basketball game attended (yes, they won), homework completed, and my son is now in bed, and I'm awaiting the next day to do it all over again.

Life was rather hectic through my only child's middle school and high school years. Try balancing your full-time career and your son's full-time career. Oh yes! My son had a full-time career all through middle school and high school and now in college. Between actual school, in season and out of season sports, balancing his life with mine was like having four full time jobs. I had to adjust my crown many times and through many tears. There were many, "I can't do this by myself", "I need help", "This is too much". But God never let me give up. And going one step further, my son never seen not one tear or moment of "give up".

My son was in middle school when I started my official career in the car business. A career that would change mine and his life forever. I had been on a job for 5 years. It was a good paying job, but I knew that there had to be more to life. So, I had to make a Queen decision, as a mommy, when I got offered the job that I applied for to sell cars. Everyone thought that I was crazy for coming off of my comfortable job and walking in to the unknown. Did I say everybody? Oh ok, just checking. I understood where they were coming from. I had just come from a bad place in my life. My crown had been completely broken. But I picked all of those pieces up and put them back together. So, when I finally got to a content place where my life seemed to be coming back together again, they were like "why do you want to disrupt that?" The answer is, I knew that there was more to life than that, and I was determined to find it. I was tired of being in a box. Getting a $.50 raise here and $1.00 there. To some, that may be a lot and may benefit you greatly. To me, a queen out here raising a king, that was nothing. If I was going to present myself as a queen, I needed to live like one. And not just that. I had a goal for my son. He was definitely going to college. My goal for him was to go to college, and scholarships or not, to come out either two ways, debt free or with very minimal loans. The dreams and the goals that I had were way bigger than my paycheck. So, at this point, it was time to queen. It was time for me to find a career and not just have a job.

After being the top salesperson in my store for months, I was promoted to Sales Manager. I was all hyped about this new career path and this new journey that I was on. Little did I know how much time this would take out of my life. I went from a normal 8-4 to 8 - whenever. So, my queening went into overdrive. I still had to mommy; I don't care what else was going on in my life. Momming was always my first ministry. I would work 10, 12, 16 hours per day. I would either leave work to pick my son up from basketball/football practices or schedule a ride for him, and then go back to work. I would make sure I was at every single game even if I had to leave and go back to work. Yelling my heart out from the stands so that everyone knew that Mommy was in the building! Keeping up on parent/teacher emails and meetings. Making sure his homework was finished. Keeping him grounded and embedded in the principles of God. And if I can tell the whole truth and nothing but, many of our dinners were take-out. There were a lot of pizza boxes in a week. And sometimes it got a little overwhelming, and my crown would tip a little. But I was determined to never let it fall off again.

I had some big heels to fill. You see, I was the first black woman Sales manager at the dealership where I worked. Can you say Queening? Ok? Two snaps of the finger with a neck tilt, "Yassss hunty!" So yes, I had some serious heels to fill. Being the first "Black Queen" in that position, the big heels that I had to fill were none other than my own. From month to month, I proved myself with record numbers. As a matter of fact, my slogan was "Prove them Wrong". I wanted to be someone that my son could proudly look up to. Most sons are mama's boys, but when it comes to business, they look up to their father's. My son definitely looked up to his dad. He has taught our son great aspects in the business world as a business owner himself. I wanted to give our son something to look up to as well. Our children already look to us as superheroes. I know to my son, even in his college days now, he looks at me as invincible, untouchable, knows everything, can take anything, and never cries. Yup, that would categorize me as a superhero. As a superhero, I have one superpower, and that would be momming! When even after a long shift at work and giving everything to everyone else you can still come home and give your child everything that you have left. That's a superpower. Sometimes my superhero outfit consist of four-inch stilettos and a blazer, and sometimes it consists of sweatpants, and oversized hoodie and some Jordan 1's. Either way, when I step out, I stay ready to queen and mommy!

You don't have to be perfect. You just have to be the best you that you can be. Never compare your size crown to someone else's. You each are on different levels in your journey. Queening is not a competition. It's an affirmation. An affirmation that you can be whoever you want to be. And guess what? Whether you have one child like me or 5 kids, they will love you regardless. There will be times that you don't feel like a queen. There will be times that you feel like you suck at momming. Get out of your head! I guarantee that when those big, bright eyes of those children look up at you, it changes everything. They don't see wrongs. When my son looks at me, he sees strength, hope, prayers, love, peace, and comfort. There are times that my son will come in my bedroom and lay across my bed just to be close to me, and he is grown now. When he is having a bad day, he will FaceTime me because he says just talking to me gives him strength and joy.

Even when you don't feel like you're queening, you are. Even when you don't feel like you're momming, you are. God has entrusted us, women, with a wonderful gift. Motherhood. We are caregivers. Our love that we give is unconditional. We are housekeepers, cooks, bakers, doctors, nurturers, providers, friends, guides, teachers and Queens.

So, one more time for the road. Two snaps of the finger, a neck tilt to the side, and screaming "Yassss hunty!" Let's keep momming and queening!

About Tee Hubbs

Tamyra "Tee Hubbs" Hubbard is an author, liturgical dancer, poet and Christian rap artist that uses creative speaking as an outlet to express of her feelings and thoughts. Her two poems, *She vs me* and *Scream*, both featured on her Rachel's Tomb album, have been streamed all across the country. Tee started writing poetry 25 years ago when she wrote her first poem "Only Human" for a school project. After a great response from classmates and being encouraged to read it in front of the class, Tee knew that she had found her niche. Over the years, she has been embedded in her first ministry, her only son. Her ultimate goal in life was to make sure he stayed on the right path with God.

Tee is a Free spirit with a slight quirkiness, and likes being "The Weirdo". Tee is a missionary that enjoys going into the trenches of third world countries and helping to rebuild and spread the love of Jesus. She has also published her first book SHE vs. ME and is currently co-authoring on an anthology, Courage to be Free. Tee boldly lives by "Stand for something or fall for anything" and "You don't know that you don't know until you know you don't know." Tee stands strongly for her faith in Jesus. You can find Tamyra "Tee Hubbs" Hubbard on the following social medica platforms.

IG: @tee_hubbs
Facebook: Tee Hubbs

<u>Favorite scriptures:</u>
Psalm 34:4, Philippians 4:6 and Mathew 6:26-34.

<u>Quote to live by:</u>
"Control Love. Don't let Love control you" ~Tee Hubbs

Rookie Mistake: It Stops with Me

By Heather L. Duma

I gazed lovingly out of my kitchen window as my six-foot-tall high school sweetheart of a husband, and my tussled-haired little lanky blue-eyed boy of a son made their way outside together, hand in hand, to play in the warm afternoon sun. Long, confident strides took my husband right to his old baseball glove. He gave it a squeeze, and a grin danced across his face. The glove looks worn, well-loved, and slides on his hand just right. "Want to play catch?" he asked our son. Squeals of "YES!" filled the air.

The excitement was palpable. I felt the warm fuzzy feelings of love and remembered being so thankful for my two beautiful men. But, suddenly, my feelings shifted to an unexplainable heaviness. A deep sigh came over me as I threw the kitchen towel over my shoulder and placed the now dried plates in the cupboard. That was such a sweet moment. But, what was this sense of dread that had come over me?

The next day would be the start of t-ball season, and you see, I was not exactly a fan of this idea. But, for some reason, a few weeks back, I felt a mysterious parental obligation to encourage our son to explore other hobbies. My head told me it was a healthy thing to do, but I would get so anxious whenever I thought about it. I brushed it off to being worried that my sweet boy would get trampled or hurt. He's my one and only. Momma bear instincts tell me to protect him at all costs. If I could put him in a bubble, I would. Kidding but....not really.

After a few more dishes had been placed in their assigned spots, my gaze drifted back to the window, and I heard, "Okay, let's go!" The t-ball practicing was about to begin! Deciding that this was a moment I didn't want to miss, I threw on my yard shoes and headed outside to cheer them along. My husband threw me a spare glove and asked me if I wanted to join in. Well, I'm more of the deck myself out with glitter and bows type, but being a boy mom has forced me out of my comfort zone. "Sure, I said!" Our son was thrilled. I slipped on the glove, and a feeling of familiarity sent a shiver down my spine.

We gently tossed the ball back and forth to one another in a triangle. When my husband threw the ball to me, he gave me a prodding little "let's see what you are made of" challenge of a toss. The ball struck my old, ragged glove right on the palm of my hand. The sound of a tightly grasped ball filled the air. And as if riding a bike again after two decades, my body instinctively snapped into posture. I threw the ball back with a "don't test me" kind of throw. With a surprised look on his face, he said, "Oh, yeah - you played a few seasons of softball, didn't you?" "No," I snipped. My body flushed with heat, and inner turmoil boiled within.

I took a few deep breaths to steady myself. My son had started catching the easy lobs, and we gently started to increase the difficulty of the throw with each new achievement. He was excited but also getting more nervous about the ball. He began to lean away from it instead of into it for that perfect catch. "Lean into it!" I said with fervor. He said, "But, it's scary!" I said,

"No, it's not! There is no need to be scared! Step to the ball and get that glove up!" When I looked into his eyes, I could see the surprise on his face. This was not typical of my normal behavior, and he looked confused. I could see that this was starting to be not so fun for him.

It was at this moment that I realized that I was unconsciously repeating an old toxic generational pattern. *I was negating my son's feelings.* There I was, feeling heated and triggered from the way I had been "taught how to play" ball, while also repeating the patterns that had led me to quit. Ouch.

I immediately walked over to my son, got on my knee, and looked at him in the eyes. "Hey, bud. I made a mistake with what I just said. I should not have invalidated your feelings about being scared of the ball. The truth is, it CAN be scary sometimes! And you know what, mommy was scared of the ball, too, when I was your age." "Really?" he said curiously. "Really! And, I want t-ball to be FUN for you! Your feelings will always be your feelings. If we stick with this, the ball might feel less scary someday. And that day is not today. And that's okay. I hear you. I love you." He gave me a quick, "Okay, mommmmmm," and asked if we could get to the fun part already - the batting! I left the boys to their batting plans and went inside to process what had just happened. Was I being triggered? The old familiar feelings. The flash of heat. The blurting out of sayings not typical of me.

Memories of a voice from the past come back to me. "We really need to toughen you up - put some hair on that chest." I closed my eyes to shake the memory but was instead transported back to a flash vision of little 8-year-old me - blonde ponytail, clear glitter jelly sandals, a Mariah Carey tee shirt with matching sticker earrings. An out-of-place silver bat was suspended over my right shoulder. I was preparing for another hit. I kept jumping out of the way of the ball. I was scared. "LEAN INTO IT,

HEATHER. Don't be a puss! You will never learn this if you keep jumping out of the way. What's the worst that could happen? You get hit? So what? It's no big deal. You just move on. Now - GET IN FRONT OF THE BALL THIS TIME."

With all the courage I could muster, I kept my eyes on the ball and swung without jumping. Except - this ball was not lobbed at me to be able to hit it. No, its path was directed straight at me. THUD. I fell to the ground in agony. Agony from a bit of pain but more from the agony of the heart. "There. It's over now. You've been hit. Now you can stop being such a pussy."

I never played ball again. And to be honest, I had not thought about this moment for decades. Now, here I was, reliving an eerily similar scenario out with my own child. Same age. Same crystal blue eyes. Same tender heart. Minus the Mariah Carey obsession, sadly.

This was just WILD to me! I had separated from the toxicity decades ago and had been, for years, only surrounded by love and light. And yet, my natural response was to spout off the same rhetoric that was shouted at me in this situation. "Lean into it! THERE IS NOTHING TO BE AFRAID OF," I said. It was like it was almost instinctive. And, that's from someone who has worked very hard to distance themselves from any old negative patterns... Ouch again.

This story serves as an oversimplification of a more powerful analogy that I feel represents a piece of parenting philosophy of many moms I admire. They keep tabs on old toxic patterns to ensure they are not being repeated. They don't want to unintentionally repeat generational patterns of negativity, invalidation, and any other myriad of negative parenting patterns. We can't avoid our negative memories and traumas. We have to uproot them to identify them, and we have to put in the work!

We have to do the work, so our children won't have to.

Momming and Queening can be a heavy weight to balance. And we do it with grace and strength. And, with all of the external focus pulling on our attention in the new Millennium, we have to be sure we are not losing sight of this important fact! We can't let heavy workloads, social media, or demanding lives keep us too busy to realize that we have deep work to do!

As each person's life story is so different, this will be unique to you. Perhaps you need to work through generational urges and repeated patterns with anger. Or addiction. Or negativity of the mind. Or of moving toward allowing the Lord to lead your family.

It's always best to seek the guidance of a trained professional. But, as a momma who is working hard to earn her crown, and with the thought that this may be helpful, I humbly share my top three ways of ensuring that I am constantly reflecting and identifying potential generational patterns that I could be unintentionally allowing to be repeated.

1. ID potential negative generational patterns and commit to turning them around. Reflect and investigate your own patterns. **Align** yourself with professionals, counselors, mentors, and/ or spiritual leaders who specialize in any negative experiences you may have faced in your past. Get yourself around the best of the best! Get a counselor, life coach, and/or an accountability partner! Find support groups such as Al-Anon. Find a few prayer sisters or trusted allies.

2. Set the new intention and **emerge** with baby steps. Get real with yourself. Identify areas that could be better or need improvement. Cut off negative relationships. Say NO to extra things that life throws at you. Say YES to this important work. Set up meetings with your new alignments

and stick with them! Track your progress. This is where you put in the work, but this is also where you start to notice the new growth.

3. Enjoy the fruits of your labor! Reflect often. Seek continued support—check in on your progress. Get alone with yourself. Get into the Word. Admit when you are wrong or when you mess up. Try, try again. Celebrate! **Bloom!**

We are capable of BLOOMING into something truly amazing! And our children serve as the next generation of beautiful little buds. The trick is - we can't let ourselves get overly busy to the point where we lose track of this very important goal. We have to do the pruning so they can flourish in the next season.

And as Pastor Mark Bunting of Emmanuel Wesleyan Church in Salisbury, Maryland, said at our son's dedication, "May our ceilings be our children's floors." For that's genuinely what Momming and Queening are all about. To ensure that where we elevate - is where our children START so that they can rise even higher.

About Heather L. Duma

Heather L. Duma is a #1 Amazon international bestselling author as well as an award winning performer, speaker, and community advocate. Driven to inspire others through the written word, Heather focuses her inspiration on the areas of family, faith, lifestyle, and how they parallel with nature, relationships, and personal growth.

After graduating at the top of her class while studying English Literature at UMES, she went on to graduate with a M.A. in Communication from The Johns Hopkins University. She now uses her passion as a writer in her day to day role as a marketing strategist. As a former public servant and fundraiser with a passion for volunteerism, Heather has also been the recipient of various national, state, and local awards for community service.

A proud Eastern Shore of Maryland native, Heather has a love for both Christian and country music having recorded her own album, performing internationally in France and Germany, and even once serving as the opening act for country music legend, Travis Tritt.

Heather resides in Hebron, Maryland with her high school sweetheart, Rob and their son, James.

Connect with Heather at:

www.heatherlduma.com

https://www.facebook.com/heatherlduma

Proof that I am Mommying and Queening

By Chevron McDonald

F irst and Foremost, I would like to Thank God for this opportunity. I never thoughtin a million years that I would be a featured author in a book. Without Him, none of this would be possible. Mommying and Queening... Do those terms even relate? Becoming a mom means less of yourself and more of the kids, right? Well, my life story involves biological kids, inherited kids, and then there's me...

The year 2003 was a start to many adventures in my life because that's the year I became a mother. Yes, I have an 18-year-old son. Ending my first year of college was tough, but perseverance was the key. I had to prove to many that despite being a young mother, I would finish college and become someone I was proud of in life. I managed to graduate college in 3 years and a quarter from Louisiana Tech University in Ruston, Louisiana, which operates on the quarter system instead of semesters.

For two whole years, I only saw my son on weekends. That was one of the many sacrifices that I made to guarantee that I would get a college degree despite the choices I made. As a parent, we are willing to take "one or two for the TEAM" to ensure that our babies are given the best opportunities in life… Proof that I am "Mommying and Queening!"

One week after I graduated college with my B.S in Psychology, I married my highschool sweetheart. Seems like a fairytale, huh? Well, that story is still being written. I'mnot going to lie; the relationship has not always been easy. We have had our share of ups and downs along the way. The saying holds a lot of truth in our relationship, "We are not perfect by a long shot, but we are perfect for each other." We are just two imperfect people that happen to be perfect for each other. Seven months after being married, we welcomed our second child. Reality then set in that I had no idea what I was going to do with a degree in Psychology. At first, I wanted to go back to school to get my Master's in School Psychology. I began to search for colleges that offered that particular degree. What I found was that only two colleges offered that program, and they were not local. I would have to leave my family once again. So, I put my life on hold for an entire year trying to figure out what it was that I could do. I knew that I needed to do something to help my husband, who put his schooling on hold to supportour family. I know somewhere in the bible it mentions that the man is supposed to be the head of household and provide for his family. However, I have always been and tosome degree still am independent, not liking to depend on others to take care of me. Besides, I had two little reasons to get up and find and walk towards my purpose. So, Idid just that. Although not using my degree, I became a substitute teacher… Once again. proving that I am "Mommying and Queening."

Being a substitute teacher would start the journey of my teaching career and my purpose and passion in life. I started out as a substitute teacher which led to a long-term substitute position for an entire school year. Being a long-term substitute made me inquire about becoming a teacher. My early thoughts of becoming a teacher meant weekends, holidays, and summers off, which meant I would be off when my kids were off. (Just to let you non-teaching folks know; teaching is so much more). God knows the plans for our life before we were even formed in our mother's womb. "For I know the plans I have for you, declares the Lord "plans to prosper you and not to harm you, plans to give you hope and a future." ~Jeremiah 29:11.

In 2007, I received my teaching certification and became certified to teach 4th-8th grade math. Teaching meant I would inherit more kids. Teaching is not a regular 9 to 5 job. When I became a teacher, I became much, much more such as: therapist, counselor, nurse, motivator, mentor, role model, disciplinarian, and their school mom. Do you realize, once children start going to school, how much time they spend with their teachers? That is something to think about. This is one of the reasons that made me evaluate myself as a teacher and my role in my students' lives. Teaching can be very rewarding, but it also can be very challenging. Sometimes, I question myself asking, "Why did I become a teacher?" Then I am quickly reminded, this is my calling from God. He ordained this, that is my why. Teachers teach more than just their subject-specific skills. It's the life-long lessons that teaches the kids, and sometimes the lessons the kids teach me, that helps me stay focused and walk in my purpose. It's the proof that I am "Mommying and Queening" for me!

There is a constant battle between my school kids and my own kids. It's a balancing act… "The Battle of Both Worlds".

Some days, I come home physically and mentally drained because every day I give all I have at school which then leaves nothing to offer my own kids. Let's rewind for a minute. My husband and I, now, have 4 kids. As the story unfolded, I didn't mention along the way that we had two more children. My oldest is an 18-year-old son followed by 3 girls, 14, 10, and 1 ½ years old. Yes, I know, I started completely over with the last one. "What was I thinking?" was my initial thought. I have to admit though, she has been one of the most precious blessings God could have given me. Being older, this experience has truly been breathtaking. It seems like she was the missing puzzle piece to our family.

My kids demand a lot of my attention. So, I really don't have time to be tired, frustrated, stressed, mentally, and physically drained when I get home from school. My kids do not want to hear, "I don't feel like it because my students took everything I had today!" The first thing they would say is, "Well, that's not my fault!" or "That's not fair to us!" or "So, when will we get our time?" Not to mention, my 1 ½ year old that just simply doesn't understand. So, most of the time I suck it up, and put on my big girl panties as some would say. I make time for them and do whatever it is that they need me to do such as: cook a meal or go pick up something to eat from a fast food restaurant (I do that a lot), comb hair, help with homework, take them to basketball practice, go to the store, listen to one of their , help them solve a problem, give them advice, do a TikTok with them, play a game, or just simply listen to whatever it is that they need to say because they just want to talk. You know, all the things that moms do!

Guess what? At school, I am always going to do my job as far as teaching the math skills (or reteaching math skills to the students that didn't get it the first time), but what else am I doing? Listening to their stories, giving advice, correcting behaviors, and whatever else duties I have that are given by the school leadership team. Sounds familiar? Sounds like mommying and queening to me.

I don't always have all the answers, and I don't always know exactly what to say at certain times, but I do know that every day I strive to be the best I can be at home as well as at school. As stated earlier, that is not always an easy task. Sometimes I feel that I don't do a good job because it takes a lot of work and dedication for both. Finding a balance is very important.

To be honest, I am still working on balancing my home life and school life. It's a constant struggle because I am always striving to do a good job in both areas. I am constantly told that I do a good job, but deep down inside I don't always feel like I do. I guess because I see my kids make mistakes or do something that they know is wrong and have been addressed. Or when my students don't always pass the tests of skills that I know they should have mastered, or when I step out of the room and expect them to behave a certain way, but they act like they have no classroom management skills. I'm not looking for validation from anyone or a pat on the back, but at the end of the dayI just want my students to be able to look back and know they had a teacher that truly cared about them and their success. I also want my own kids to know their mom loves them and have their best interest at heart. I strive to give them the best of me every single day, and when they are all grown up, I hope they will know that I have done the best I could at raising them to be not only productive citizens but prosperous adults.

After taking care of my family and giving my students my all, you may wonder, where is the time for my self-care? Making time for myself is the hardest struggle of all. Sometimes, I feel like I get too caught up in my job as a teacher and my role as a mom and wife that I don't make time for myself. Time for my kids, time for my students, time to be a wife, and time for myself is a balancing act. However, I wouldn't trade my life for any other because my kids, whether biological or inherited, are a gift from God. I am realizing that it's not going to always be a perfect scenario, and I have to be reminded that they are kids. They have room for error and improvement, and it's my job to make sure they learn from their mistakes and progress.

I'm so glad I get to be a part of shaping their lives. I am constantly speaking positivity in their lives and letting them know that despite every situation they face or will face that God says, they will have more than they can contain. Growing up with a praying grandmother and being very involved in church, allows me to instill in my kids that nothing is possible without God. We are blessed because God in heaven is our Father and the heir to our inheritance. Blessed be the God and Father of our Lord Jesus Christ, who hath blessed us with all spiritual blessings in heavenly places in Christ. ~Ephesians 1:3. Being married is a privilege and learning to love someone's imperfections is a gift.

Lastly, making the time for my sanity is much needed. I was told long before I knew what it meant that I would never fit in. Just two years ago, I finally realized what that really meant. Doing things that you know are not in the will of God to try and fit in landed me in a place of deep hurt which I channeled through anger, but lessons become blessings.

The devil tried to destroy me by attacking people that I loved, especially my son. But God has a way of showing us that we give the devil too much credit. Because of situations I have faced, I, now, have a stronger relationship with God. I am nowhere near where I want to be, but I do Thank God for where he is taking me. I realize my time with my family at home and time withmy students helps me stay sane. I do from time to time take a break from both. I have also been told that there is a promotion in the future for me, and God knows I am waiting on it. However, being in the classroom with my inherited kids is enough for me right now because it seems like it's right where I need to be. So, I'll continue to figure out on a day-by-day basis how I will balance my time between the many kids I have inherited as a teacher and the four children I birthed, but this, too, is proof that I'm killing this thing called "Mommying and Queening."

About Chevron McDonald

Chevron McDonald is a graduate of Louisiana Tech University where she received a bachelor's degree in psychology. She also received a MED in Curriculum and Instruction from Concordia University-Portland. She is currently a 5th grade math teacher in Baton Rouge, LA. She has been teaching for 14 years. To her teaching isn't an easy task, but she feels it is her calling, her purpose in life, sometimes frustrating, keeps her busy, even anxious and tired, but it's what she loves to do and is a part of her everyday life. Her hope is that she touches at least one of her students in such a way that will impact their lives leaving a lasting impression for a lifetime; one in which the students themselves know their purpose in life. Raised in a small town called Coushatta, LA , she loves being outside and hanging out with family and friends. Being a basketball mom is one of her favorite and most rewarding job.

Knock, Knock Motherhood! It's me, Linda.

By Linda Flores

To know my story about being a parent in present day society, you need to first go to where most stories start, at the beginning. My story begins in the spring of 2008 in Minot, North Dakota, I had just received the news that my path to motherhood was going to be difficult and possibly not even an option for me. I was about to complete my enlistment with the United States Air Force, and at 23 years old I wasn't prepared to process that information. I was not ready to have kids that very moment or even close to having a family, but I had already planned in my head what that chapter of my story would look like.

I wanted a large family with at least four kids. I, myself, have one sibling, but I am part of a rather large extended family. Growing up, my sister and my cousins were my best friends; my confidants, and I wanted that for my future family. I was given all the information and different options I had available to me, but it felt after each option was presented, my perfect family was slipping through my imaginary fingertips, and the tighter I held on, the faster they disappeared. I took all the information and reminded myself that although it would be a hard, almost impossible journey, I had to keep my faith and trust in the Lord to guide me.

I will admit I struggled with patience and my faith, I let doubt and uncertainty take over my mind those days. Unable to see past the large, concrete, double steel wall in my head that had the biggest letters that read "It will never happen". I only told a few individuals because I was embarrassed, and sad. Honestly, I still didn't really allow myself to process what that diagnosis actually meant for me. Of the few people I did tell, I had one friend without any hesitation offer her womb if I ever needed it. Just that gesture alone reminded me that God was showing me that He was hearing my prayer. Even though at the time, I could hardly hear it, but it also showed me that I needed to trust the process. I can never thank her enough for her selfless act and how much faith and hope that one gesture gave me. She broke down that impenetrable wall in my mind forever.

Unexpected News!

Fast forward to 2010, I was working at a job that required me to be very active, I was eating healthy, and just enjoying my life, not knowing that in April I was going to get the shock of my life. The day I found out I was pregnant was a normal day. I didn't feel sick (yet). I was a few days late in my cycle which for the most part was not odd, but I felt like I had to take a test just in case.

I did my normal routine that day and while I was at the grocery store, I decided to get a test. After bringing up what felt like 300 pounds of groceries to my second story apartment, I took the test and waited. I thought it would be like all the others before, and I refused to give any hope to that small plastic test sitting on my counter in the bathroom. My heart was already prepared to give me the sadness that would happen right after my eyes focused on the results. However, my eyes could not believe what they were seeing. My heart felt like it stopped, and I realized I was holding my breath. Right in front of me was a bright blue plus sign! I fell to my knees and thanked God for allowing me to have my blessing. Of course, I did what most women do in this situation; I went to the store and bought a few more, well actually I bought several more. Each test brought me more joy and excitement. I immediately scheduled an appointment to confirm what all those tests were telling me. At my first doctor's appointment, I anxiously waited to hear the good news from my doctor. After a quick test, I was sitting in a cold exam room trying my hardest not to shake. When the doctor came in, she had a serious look on her face. I was no longer shaking; my body was like a stone statue already prepared for the news even if my heart wasn't. She informed me that the test said I was not pregnant. I said, "Okay, thank you," with what felt like an endless supply of tears forming in my eyes. I left so fast out of the office, I would have given the flash a run for his money. I cried for what felt like hours in my car that afternoon. So many questions without any logical answers kept swimming in my head. Why? Did I not have enough patience? Did I want it too much? Once home, I had suppressed everything and only showed that I was a little disappointed. A few weeks had passed from that doctor's appointment. I had been slowly trying to get back to "normal," trying to convince myself that I, indeed, was not pregnant, but my body had different plans. I began to feel sick all the time, and I was not feeling myself, so I thought just maybe the doctor was wrong.

So again, I took a test, and once again it came out positive. I thought, how could this be? What has changed? I scheduled an appointment with a different doctor and asked for a blood test this time around. Like the previous visit, there I was waiting to see if there was a life growing inside me, but this time I was on guard there was no smile on my face, there were no expectations. The doctor came in and she immediately said "Congratulations!" I think she thought I didn't hear her because she said it again, but I couldn't move or speak. It was after a few moments that I felt the smile return on my face, tears were sliding down my cheeks, but they were tears of joy. I was finally going to have the one thing I, honestly, thought wasn't going to be possible. I was going to be a Mom!

Motherhood meets Post-Partum Depression

Alexander Lucas Flores came into this world via C-section on December 9, 2010 at an impressive 9 pound 7 ounces. He was perfect, I finally was ready to be a Mom or so I thought. Post-Partum depression is so sneaky. I was a first-time mom. My son had Colic. Sleep was a distant memory. Everything just felt so difficult to do. The motherly instincts didn't seem to kick in. I did not know I even had any form of depression until a supervisor of mine brought it to my attention. (I should add that I went back to work less than four weeks after I had Alexander).

Being a first-time parent, I had no reference on just how much my life was going to change. I thought I would just bounce back and would not need to adjust much in my life, but as most parents know, I was completely wrong. Adding post-partum depression into the mix only made things harder. I had many thoughts going through my mind, constantly. I remember one thought that played like a broken record in my mind. Was I really supposed to be a mom? Then, the other doubting questions swam in my head adding to my doubt. Did I make a mistake? What kind of mom am I going to be for him? Then you throw social media into the mix, and for me, it was exceedingly difficult not to compare myself to the other parents. You don't want to look flawed in any way.

So many people don't see the struggle that comes with parenting. All we see and show, myself included, are the smiles, and the best photos possible. Alexander wasn't even three months old yet, and I already felt like a failure. I had no idea it was the depression talking. I just thought and was told from multiple people that it was normal. I'm just a new mom. Once I sought the help I needed, my gray world full of doubt and negativity transformed to color once again and brought a new perspective to this whole parenting gig. I realized that I needed to give myself a break from my own judgement and instead focus on what was right in front of me. My brand-new, beautiful, baby boy.

Motherhood meets the opinion of others

I do admit even now, 10 years later, I still doubt myself. I don't think that ever goes away, but what I do know is that what works for me and my family, doesn't necessarily work for others, and that is perfectly okay. So, to all the new moms out there reading this now, it does get easier. You will find your groove, and you will look back and laugh at what you felt was so difficult was actually the easy part of parenting. One of the toughest parts, so far, in my journey as a parent was finding out Alexander would be an only child. That "plan" I thought up when I was 23 about having a big family just wasn't going to happen. I struggled, silently, for years unwilling to share what was going on in my life. Again, from the embarrassment and sadness.

For a good four or five years, I was always being asked when I was going to have another child. That I better not wait too long, or Alexander would not be able to bond with a sibling. I was even asked if I felt guilty that he was all alone. I know most of these people who shared their thoughts were asking more out of curiosity, and I couldn't blame them because on the outside I looked and acted as if everything was perfect. They were saying statements that I had already asked myself a million times. I wish my body would have worked a little better for a little longer, but unfortunately, it wasn't meant to be.

Social Media: A Love-Hate Relationship

I have a love-hate relationship with all the many different social media outlets. Living far from my family and friends for many years, I loved the fact that I could stay up to date on all the current events in their lives, but it was and actually still is hard to see all the wonderful pregnancy/baby announcements. There is always that tugging on my heart and that thought of, "Why can't it be me?" Then, there is that guilt again of, "I have my son. I should be happy with that, and let it go." However, when the option to have more kids gets taken away from you, and you have absolutely no other choice because your health means more, then it's a lot harder to process. So, if you see a newlywed couple or a couple with no kids, as exciting as it is to ask when the kids are coming, sometimes, it's better to wait, and let the couple tell you themselves. We really don't know what struggles they may be having behind closed doors. Or, if they only have one child, like me, think twice about asking if more kids are coming. We might not have the option, or maybe some may know in their hearts that one was all they needed.

Motherhood and today's Technology

As I said earlier, Alexander was born in 2010. I was that parent that was dead set on him being raised with strict rules on technology. I wasn't going to allow to any screen time, and he was not going to get a phone until he was in high school. I am laughing as I write this now. I didn't follow any of my rules. Not a single one. He has had a cell phone since he was eight. He started off with a kids' tablet and has now upgraded to his very own Virtual Realty system. He loves watching The Simpsons, and I think he can be considered an expert on The Simpsons trivia. I do only have one child, and I hate to admit it but sometimes that show or that game he is playing interests him more than mom. I need a break every once in a while, so I will let him have his technology entertainment a little more than most.

In the ever-so-changing fast paced world of technology that we live in, I feel like we are the pioneering parents on how to handle the balance of technology with these young minds. Even school, especially now, amid the pandemic, everything is done from a computer. I have had many conversations with many different individuals from all walks of life. Some told me, it was too much, that he would fall behind in school. Some said they didn't agree with what I allowed. I acknowledged what they said, and the beauty of all of that is I chose what I want to hear or not. Everyone is entitled to their opinion and trust me everyone will have an opinion on what is best for your child. At the end of the day, you live with that child, and you can see what is best. I, personally, just keep an open mind and heart, knowing that when people do share their thoughts, for the most part, they are coming from a loving place. I can use or not use their suggestions. I know for my household I try my best to balance his technology with his daily life. He has to accomplish certain tasks before he can dive into his gaming activities. He has daily chores which involve something simple like sweeping the kitchen to a slightly more complex chore such as washing his own laundry. With those set parameters, he can learn how to balance his work and play. I don't see technology slowing down any time soon so I choose to teach him now so he can have a solid foundation when he ventures out to make his own life. Something I try my best to follow is putting as many child safety settings as I can, since everything is now readily available at his fingertips. I want him to take his time growing up, he deserves a chance to enjoy being a kid because it is such a short time in our lives. I learned early on that he was very curious and tried to search for answers on his own. Of course, he didn't realize that the search engine he was on didn't know he was 6. As for now, he is a straight A student. He loves to read, and I make sure he has a stack of books every week readily available to him. Some might say that it's too much, and some might say I'm not doing enough, but it is what works for my house, and that is the exact point I'm trying to make. Never feel guilty on what you feel is best for your child.

Even Superwoman Needs Self-Care

Speaking of opinions, I think it's safe to say that most moms in the beginning give 100 percent of themselves to their new baby and nothing else. Partly because we are so tired, it's almost impossible to function past the baby. What I think happens after a while is we get use to that role and forget that we are individuals as well. I know I'm not the only one who believes we really are superheroes. We have careers, homes, and families to take care of, and we do it without complaining or reward. With all of that on our plate, it doesn't surprise me that when it comes to thinking of ourselves, we tend to let guilt be the guiding factor. I was guilty of exactly that for many years. I can admit now that I do regret not allowing myself time for just me. When you have so much going on around you, it's hard to see what you hope for yourself and for your future. For us moms, all that matters in time is now. Instead, you are planning your child's future. making sure they have the best one possible. Don't get me wrong that should be thought of regardless, but if you don't take the steps early to take care of yourself, mind, body, and soul, you will eventually realize that you can't give your best self to your kids, years down the road because it is no longer there. Remember to take care of yourself. Do something for yourself. It doesn't even have to be something big or some elaborate day. It can be something as simple as having thirty minutes of uninterrupted time to do whatever you want without the kids. It could be focused on fitness and going for a walk or run. For myself, it's my hair. I see my wonderful hairstylist every 2 months. That is my own time to be focused on just me, no outside interruption. It's where I can relax, vent, and do something that is just for me. I think it is important to keep giving ourselves goals or tasks that we do just on our own so that we do not lose ourselves and can still give our families our absolute best selves.

Motherhood: A life's journey

I have held the Mom title for ten years, and I know I have so much to learn in this lifelong journey. I think back to my 23-year-old self with the perfect family plan and can smile knowing now that God had such a better plan for me. If I could go back 10 years and give myself advice, I would say don't be so hard on yourself; quit comparing yourself to others. You do not have to struggle alone; find your village. It could be your family or the parents on your kid's soccer team. Lastly, have faith and enjoy the journey, it goes by so fast.

About Linda Flores

Linda Flores lives in El Paso, Texas. She is a devoted mother to her ten-year-old son, Alexander. She is a proud Veteran and served in the United States Air Force. She has a passion for helping in her community from her work in law enforcement as well as medical assisting to participating in donation organizations and also spreading random acts of kindness as much as she can around her community. She enjoys her family time and loves a good adventure. In her spare time, she loves to read and has yet to find a book she hasn't liked.

It's Okay to NOT be Okay

By Gloria Corral

ood moms have scary thoughts. I sat on my bed holding my fourth precious baby, so in love and overjoyed, yet tears began running down my face. I, physically, felt like I was drowning. My heart was racing, and I felt like I couldn't catch my breath. Why did I feel a storm cloud over my head? Why were my thoughts centered on fear and despair? I couldn't help but wonder if this was the effect of a pandemic. Could it be a hormonal imbalance? I began to have physical symptoms of anxiety, and in a nutshell, my anxiety was giving me anxiety. How and why did this happen? Motherhood felt beautifully overwhelming.

A few years ago, I miscarried twice back-to-back. It was absolutely heartbreaking. The agony of holding onto what could be and what wasn't was suffocating. I cried in the car. I cried as I buried my face in my pillow. I shut down, and we didn't share our heartbreaking news with anyone. It felt like it was a whirlwind of emotions, and I felt inadequate. Like rapid fire, I was stumbling into loneliness. I provided a slew of excuses to family and friends as to why I would suddenly burst into tears. "I have a headache." I had never felt so heartbroken, hopeless and alone. I sat at work staring at my computer feeling inevitably discouraged. I frantically wanted to hold my babies in my arms. I wanted to physically kiss them a million times. I just wanted to be a mom.

I reached a breaking point - I knew I needed support from someone who knew exactly what I was going through. I sought counseling and attended an infertility support group, "The Hannah Group," at a local church. We met weekly, we shared our struggles and encouraged each other with scripture. Pregnancy loss is more common than I knew at the time, yet it was taboo to speak of it, or so I thought. 1 out of every 4 women will have experienced a form of pregnancy loss. If you are in this season, please know you are not alone, let me encourage you to renew your mind with the Lord's promises.

"but those who hope in the LORD will renew their strength."
~Isaiah 40:31

"For I am the LORD your God who takes hold of your right hand and says to you, Do not fear; I will help you."
~Isaiah 41:13

"You will keep in perfect peace those whose minds are steadfast, because they trust in you." ~Isaiah 26:3

Keep your focus on God and not on the problem. Prayers do big things. Do not feel pressured or intimidated by fancy prayers because the Holy Spirit will intercede your words for you. A heartfelt prayer is about believing big that GOD is in control, that He is sovereign, and limitless. His peace is inexplainable - his peace is one of a kind.

"The LORD will fight for you; you need only to be still."
~Exodus 14:14

Most importantly, remember that you are not alone.

"The LORD himself goes before you and will be with you; he will never leave you nor forsake you. Do not be afraid; do not be discouraged." ~Deuteronomy 31:8

After such a heartbreaking loss, I prayed and prayed, and one mighty day I began to see God speaking. I fumbled through my big orange study bible and opened it to Samuel. It read,

"And the Lord gave Hannah three sons and two daughters. Meanwhile, Samuel grew up in the presence of the Lord."
~1 Samuel 2:21 NLT

I thought, "Wait, who is Samuel? And what does any of this mean, Lord?" As I hovered over the page I glanced at bold letters that read, LISTENING. Let's pause here for a second, the creator of this world, our Sovereign GOD, the Alpha and the Omega, was literally telling me to LISTEN! Are any of us really listening? God speaks to us in so many different ways, we just have to ask for His wisdom and discernment to know and understand what it is He wants to tell us. Curiously, I flipped back a page, and I read the story of Hannah. Have you read it, friends? It struck me. In short, Hannah was yearning to be a mother and was ridiculed for not being able to conceive. She was discouraged. What did Hannah do? She left her worries at the altar and prayed fervently for a son. Her attitude then changed from complete discouragement to hope in the Lord. So, with a shattered heart, I prayed again and left it at the hands and feet of the Lord. *"This hope is a strong and trustworthy anchor for our souls. It leads us through the curtain into God's inner sanctuary."* Hebrews 6:19

I was told I could not conceive children during that time due to a tennis ball sized cyst in my uterus that would need to be surgically removed or disappear naturally. I know…intense, right? A week later, I went in for a checkup feeling very nervous and defeated. As the nurse searched for the cyst, she looked entirely baffled. I, suddenly, heard the words, "your cyst is completely gone, but…there is a BABY IN THERE!" Yep, you read that right, A BABY! Cue the tears. God gave me another chance. Can you imagine the excitement?

I love to share this story with my beautiful kids and remind them of my prayer, "Lord, my heart desires so much to be a mom, please allow me to have a baby." And, well, now I have FOUR. God blessed me with more than I could have ever imagined, and I am very thankful.

At the onset of the 2020 pandemic, we found out we were expecting our fourth baby. I was convinced I was experiencing symptoms of the virus, but no, it was actually a 10-week-old baby. Say What!!!? We were ecstatic. As my pregnancy progressed, I was concerned how I would go through this journey during a pandemic. It was a blessing, and a walk in the fire. Anxiety and crippling fear took over my thoughts. While I was beyond grateful and so excited to welcome my sweet baby, I couldn't help but worry about his birth, his health, and my health. I stopped sleeping well as I went through a million scenarios in my head. There were days where my joy was beaming, my grateful heart praised God, and I couldn't thank Him enough. Other days, everything was cloudy, it was hard to find joy and be present. I tried to quickly do anything to keep those toxic thoughts out of my mind and away from triggering my fearful anxiety. Lockdowns and virtual everything were challenging and made for lonely days. Some days were a complete scramble, I tried my hardest to make sure my little ones had enough activities at home, and quality time well spent with mom and dad. At this point, I think the entire world can relate. We tried our hardest to care for our children's mental health. I guess you could say I ignored mine.

But GOD. He provided in every way possible. Friends and family dropped by and brought meals, a sweet gift, written notes and sometimes just a good ol' wave from the car. It gave me quite the new perspective. The little things are worth so much more than we give them value. It made me so thankful for our families, and for the simplest form of face-to-face interaction with friends and strangers. My 83-year-old neighbor dropped in one morning and told me she felt it was urgent that she pray over me. She had no idea I was feeling despair and needed to hear from the Lord. Praise God for such a sweet woman. He spoke through His word and through the actions and words of others. God spoke peace and reminded me that I was in the best hands. I delivered by Midwife (The BEST!), early morning. Actually, my child arrived less than 30 mins after I arrived at the birthing center. I realllyyyy wanted a water birth, but God had other plans. It's quite comical really, my loving husband snapped a selfie to commemorate the beginning of filling the water tub only to be interrupted seconds later because it was go-time. I, literally, cried laboring, begging to get in the glorified tub. Y'all, there wasn't enough water to get my toes slightly wet. My delivery and recovery was absolutely amazing; my fourth baby was born in lightning speed, happy, healthy and oh, so adorable.

Two months postpartum, I began to experience physical symptoms of postpartum anxiety. I was in a space where I was frantically trying to "live life" and keep everyone healthy. The thought of anything happening to them was beginning to drive me to full blown panic attacks. My heart was racing, I felt like I couldn't breathe and felt as if I was physically drowning. Scary thoughts plagued my mind. Again, it became a battlefield trying to remain present and focused on good things. Postpartum anxiety disorder is real and affects 10% of new mothers. It's not limited to depression or a timeline. The onset of anxiety may begin during pregnancy, after childbirth and some women may experience postpartum anxiety after weaning the child. Postpartum anxiety is constantly worrying and experiencing feelings of dread, and can go from a state of worrying to physical symptoms. The nerve, right? It is often misdiagnosed and not discussed as often as postpartum depression.

There were many factors to consider when I began to experience extreme anxiety. I was sleep deprived, fearful of a pandemic, overwhelmed by the many to-do's on my list and my own pressure to be operating at 100%. I couldn't help but think about how much I was failing at everything. I love them all so much, who could care for them and love them like I do? Why was it hard to stop worrying some days? I felt terrified to go anywhere apart from them. I feared sudden tragedy. Was I the only one feeling this way? It really felt lonely out there. I reminded myself of the people in our lives who love my children and husband and would care for them should something happen to me, and sadly, I thought they maybe even do a better job. Hold on for a second here, while it is true that many others would help, the Lord chose me to be their mama and my husband's wife. God equips me, and I know now that I am doing an amazing job. Thank you, Lord.

My mind was going 100mph. At the end of the day, you know, when the kids are all in bed and you're laying down having "mom time" even though you should be asleep girl? Yep, during that mom time I was going in circles, thinking of all kinds of things. Did I spend good quality time with my kids? Why did I yell so much today? Why was I so impatient? Did I teach my kids enough? Were my activities really fun and educational? Was my baby getting all the proper nutrients? Did I make healthy meals? Have I spent enough time with my husband? Did I give everyone their vitamins? When's the last time I mopped the floor? What laundry load am I on? Do we need eggs? What color should we paint? Why do I feel so lonely in a home full of blessings? Raise your hand if you want me to stop already and get to the point. I felt INADEQUATE. I felt SCARED. I feared illness and death. I feared failure. I feared the opinions of man. FEAR, FEAR, FEAR.

Oh child, how many times does God tell us NOT to fear or worry? One morning, my son quickly stopped me in my tracks and said (in a *very* annoyed voice), "Mom, SERIOUSLY? AGAIN!? You are worried? Didn't we just read that in our bible story this morning, Jesus said not to worry." Well, alright then kid. You got a point.

"For God has not given us a spirit of fear and timidity, but of power, love and self-discipline." ~2 Timothy 1:7

"Don't worry about anything, pray about everything. Tell God what you need and thank for all he has done." ~Philippians 4:6

After a few months of what felt like agony, I finally feel above water. From time to time, I still get random bouts of anxiety. I dread going anywhere without my husband and kids; I just feel safe when I am with them. Thankfully, I have an amazing husband and best friend who is patient and constantly doing his best to help me. I have reached out for help and speaking out about my feelings, struggles and accomplishments. I try to get myself out there, and I have to say those little solo Target shopping trips really do put a pep in my step. We took a much needed vacation and I enjoyed rest with family. As a child, I had no idea the extent of the sacrifice and challenges my parents endured for me to be the person I am today. When I was born, my mother's circumstances were very difficult, she and I lived in a homeless shelter until I was about three months. She persevered through every challenge and I am in awe of her strength. Go, mom! I am a grown adult, and boy, I needed a good hug from my parents. Caring for my mental health is important! I am surrounding myself with help, positivity and encouragement. Every day is an opportunity for me to look up and gaze at my Lord and Savior and ask for strength, guidance and grace. *"Give all your worries and cares to God, for he cares about you."* 1 Peter 5:7

As I took the time to reflect on such a challenging time, I can't help but wonder why I put so much pressure on myself? Why is there so much pressure to have the perfect story, pregnancy, recovery, journey and mom life? "AIN'T NOBODY PERFECT BUT JESUS, Y'ALL!"

I'm identifying my triggers and ways to treat my anxiety. Sometimes you need prayer, sometimes you need medicine, sometimes you need therapy, whatever it is, Get.The.Help! I am NOT okay, all the time. I am NOT perfect, and I'm learning that is okay! For you see, in my utmost weakness, I was STRENGTHENED.

> *"My grace is sufficient for you, for my power is made perfect in weakness. Therefore, I will boast all the more gladly about my weaknesses, so that Christ's power may rest on me. That is why, for Christ's sake, I delight in weakness in insults in hardships in persecutions, in difficulties. For when I am weak, then I am strong."* ~2 Corinthians 12:9

I make mistakes and I am learning from them. The days when I feel like I totally blew it I'll ask the kids about their day and they will say they had a great day. Really kids? Did I not just turn into SHE HULK? It's just grace, y'all. What better way to teach our kids the love and grace of Jesus than our real life situations? Teaching them that sometimes we mess up, we need help, we aren't perfect, but we have a Lord and Savior that IS PERFECT, and we can do as best as we can, and that is enough. I recently asked my kids what mom does best, their answers were interesting. My oldest said I make delicious lemonade (I've made that only a handful of times), my second kiddo said I made amazing pancakes (nothing special just outta the bag), and my third looked at me so lovingly and said I was great at freaking out. Yep, she said that. She also said she loves it when mommy brings her bananas and gives her medicine. I suppose I am not so bad, right?

I recently read an amazing devotional, "Mom Set Free" by Jeannie Cunnion, and two statements resonated with me, she said, "STOP STRIVING TO BE ENOUGH." This doesn't mean, quit everything and do nothing. No, keep going girl, do your best, have fun, rejoice in the Lord, but just stop, stop striving to do everything perfectly, relying on self and running yourself ragged. His grace is enough and new in the mornings. "We need to shift our focus to our blessings and not making them burdens."

Mamas, it isn't about a perfect pregnancy and postpartum journey, or how perfect you cook that dinner you looked up on Pinterest or being the perfect PTA mom - but if you do those things perfectly, go ahead, girl. It's about knowing that it's OKAY TO NOT BE OKAY. God chose us to be the mama He knew we could be for our babies, and He promised to walk right beside us every day in our ups and downs. In the words of Maury Povich, "You are…the best mama." You do not have to have it together ALL.THE.TIME. It is okay to need help. It's okay to ask someone to hold the baby because haven't showered [in days perhaps] and need a minute. It's okay if you are struggling with something physical, mental, or emotional. It is okay. It's okay to leave the dishes in the sink and get some rest. It's okay that there's piles of clean laundry, dirty laundry and piles of outfits that don't fit anyone in almost every room, and instead of tackling them you choose to sit and eat a bowl of ice cream. Getting everything done is not impossible, I personally just can't do it every day. Like my dear friend once said, "go rest, you're not a robot." She's right. I truly can't get to it all. My mind and body need rest, and caring for my family and myself trumps laundry, unless we're all out of undies, in that case we gotta figure something out!

I started the homeschool year with a full calendar of the things I would be teaching by day. I spent so much time preparing for it. Ask me how many times I have referred to my master list, much less followed it. At this point, the kids are teaching me. Kidding. But seriously, they have learned so much. We have lived life, we have real experiences, we have had fun playing, cooking and randomly watching videos of Honey Badgers kicking behind and devouring snakes. It's not a perfect curriculum, but they are learning so much.

Let's take a stand now, to vow as of this moment, to embed in our pretty little heads that we do not need to be the perfect mom or wife. We just need to love them as we are today. Ladies, we need to be reminded that every journey is not the same, and all parenting hacks and rules do not apply to every mother. We all have strengths and weaknesses, and they are not the same. I wish I would not have allowed myself to feel pressured by society to have set rules on what anxiety, depression, miscarriage, baby sleeping, feeding and perfect routines should look like. It STRESSED ME OUT! Yea, I said it! We co-sleep, and it's the best. It's cuddly, it's also only having a crease on the bed to sleep on, but we sleep. They're happy, we're happy.

Whether you are working, stay home, married or single - whatever your walk of life, I want to encourage you to embrace your journey. Start your day by setting your gaze on Christ, seek His will, seek His help and wisdom and pray about everything. Find your village. If family is far away, find a local mom group, find the ladies that gather on the porch, find the ladies that love to hold babies or mentor other women. Fill your cup. Be honest with yourself, be vocal about your struggles. Surround yourself with positive supportive people when you are down, and when you are up, be there for those who need to be lifted and empowered. Go ahead, buy the mug that makes you feel all kinds of girly and womanly, ready to take on the day - even if you are actually just drinking chocolate milk. Whether you're rocking those arts & crafts and healthy muffin recipes or scraping some funky looking thing off the floor, wait, what is that? Should I smell it? NO, don't smell it. Give yourself a high five. When Alexa won't homeschool the kids, the crying doesn't stop, your hair has been in the same glamorous up do it's been all week, and you are eating breakfast at the table alone again, please know, I see you mama. I am walking right there with you. Whatever kind of day it is, you are doing awesome sweetie. You are fierce. You are kind, beautiful and smart.

Let's rejoice at those squishy cheeks, big hugs, and let's laugh and enjoy those precious nap times when your ninja moves are in full effect as you step away from baby. Your work is not unseen. You do not need to strive to be Wonder Woman every day, for you my darling, by the mercy of God, have created life.

On the days you forget who you are, and the stress and demands of the day are bringing you to tears, remember that God's got you, and He is very good at what he does. On a tough run-down day, with tears running down my cheeks, I said, "GOD, but I am just a mom." It was almost as if it meant nothing else. God quickly reminded me of my prayers as a young little girl, "Dear God, I pray to be a mommy when I grow up," and again as a heartbroken woman after miscarriage, "God, please. My heart hurts so much. I just want to be a mom." I am blessed and happy to report, I am JUST A MOM, and I am so grateful and so in love with my husband and my little ones. Each and every one of them with their own quirks and fascinations. I am Just a Mom, with my own identity in Christ, with my own struggles, wants and desires, and I couldn't be happier.

About Gloria Corral

Gloria Corral is a stay-at-home mother to four beautiful children and wife to an amazing hard-working husband. She is new to the field of homeschool teaching and seeking opportunities for growth. She has a Bachelor's degree in Finance from the University of Texas-El Paso (UTEP), GO MINERS, and a Master's Degree from the University of Arlington in Business Administration. Gloria retired from the Lockheed Martin Aeronautics Co. at the ripe age of 31 to pursue her career in motherhood. In her professional career, she received her Lean Six Sigma certification, and leadership excellence training. She has acquired experience in Supply Chain Management, Aircraft Sustainment, Operations, Quality, and Strategy. Gloria was a member of the Society of Hispanic Professional Engineers where the focus was on STEAM Education for students and professionals. Her joy and love of God is very important. She's a PTA mom, and "wanna-be" Pinterest mom. Gloria enjoys all things decor, salsa dancing, and a good fiesta. You can always catch her on the dance floor. Stay tuned for more adventures.

Parent of the Year

By Fasina Wilkie

And the parent of the year award goes to…me, that's who, Fasina Wilkie. Author, Wildseed Wilk. You could catch my 11-year-old son running in the street, outside the house, with his socks with a football, or taking a short cut from his bus stop, across the neighbor's roof, just to jump in our backyard to get into the house. My 20-year-old, introverted daughter avoids earthlings at all costs. She acts just like me, so we are "team bump heads." She also has a special gift with her sight. My 18-year-old niece, yes, I'm also an aunt-mom; she's a little rough around the edges. She told me the filtered water tastes too clean; she said water out of the faucet tastes better. Anyway, it's quite a special bunch, and I'm aware that I'm the culprit of all this freeness. No matter what you tell your children, they mimic different ways about you, even ways they think they don't like about you. As parents, we have the responsibility to guide these little interesting beings into independent adults. We must teach them how to function through all the hate and still be successful and happy. But did we figure it out?...

All women are queens, but to me, single mothers develop superpowers. So many roles and responsibilities, so many hats to wear, how does she find time for herself? Many people in the Black community weren't fortunate enough to be raised in two-parent loving households. Don't get me wrong, though, in most cases there was still lots of love, laughter and family. I was raised in North Philadelphia (Norf) where the entire community is one big family. I was one that was blessed to be raised with two loving parents/partners. Nonetheless, raising children often falls on one parent, usually the mom. There are several studies that have shown that over 70% of Black babies are born to single (unmarried) mothers. This, to me, raises several questions. Where's all the dignity, love, and protection for the women? Or is that not the role for every man in every religion? They are out there. It's just as easy as finding a needle in a haystack. To all my brothers that are still having a rough time getting stable mentally and financially, *I pray that you get better. I know the system was designed to tear you down and keep you down for a lifetime; still, we need you to raise up, tap into the magic, build your relationship with the creator, and respect women.*

I, myself, am a single mother. In life, I've been blessed, but adulting ain't been no crystal stairs for me. How life treats us affects how we interact with our innocent children. With my first child's father, I was fresh out of college, young; it didn't work out. He's a responsible dad, however. With my son's father, there was love, marriage, and laughter. After nine years that ended in deceit, disgust, heartache, TV/newspaper articles, and embarrass-ment. It felt like a bad dream, more like a mirage than a marriage. Have you heard the saying when it rains it pours? During this same time, I was consistently adding written reports of hateful discrimination to my FOUR Equal Employment Opportunity (EEO) cases that are still collecting dust at the U.S. Equal Employ-ment Opportunity Commission over the last five years (President Trump's entire tour) from the intense workplace bullying I endured from several management officials at the Philadelphia Social

Security Administration. This was also the period where this employer put me out of work for 10 months without pay, waiting to give me an approved reassignment under reasonable accommodation which eventually landed in a $50,000 pay cut, and an unreasonable situation. The pay cut was higher than the salary. You can be good one day, and at scratch the next. Moving forward, I still had to be a mom. Despite grieving and losing two incomes, his income and mine, my daughter was still asking me questions like, "What are we doing about my prom?" "Can you take me driving? I need to get my license before my birthday." I had to talk to my elementary age son about jail and consequences, and what "away" really means for his father. I had to talk to him about privacy, and how to respond (or not respond) if people try to pry into his little personal life. It's my job to prepare him for life. It's different out here for Black boys. It's unfortunate how early these types of conversations are happening in the Black Community. If it is one thing for certain, change is constant, and the devil don't sleep...racists either. Sometimes I feel like postpartum depression timeframes need to be reevaluated; I may be still suffering. With my devastating past, I surely needed more than a time out. I decided to focus on the lesson: *"The LORD will fight for you; you need only to be still." Exodus 14:14*

After my series of mess, I decided to be "still". What happened to my life I pondered? Racism? Relationships? It is not that simple. I think it's important to self- reflect and research your own situations to hold yourself accountable for paying attention; you don't want to keep tripping over the same rock. Life is too short for that. Do you really know what makes you happy? Being still and reflecting can help you with this. Taking one day at a time. Healing you is better than being in stagnant misery. Get a relationship with God, be thankful and pray. This will help with your inner strength. Learn how to pray for things like courage and wisdom. Get yourself right so you can continue Momming and Queening.

At times, I've been completely overwhelmed with depression. Depression is a devastating illness that affects the total being, physically, emotionally, and spiritually. When you are going through this at work, does anyone care? The expectation at work is to keep it moving. You must keep it moving with the things you love too. Do your children care? At times, it may seem like they don't. They love you and depend on you; they are a blessing. Back in the day, I remember parents saying, stay out of grown folks' business, and we listened. I don't understand how all my personal business is transparent to my children. When I was at my lowest, my girls gave me strength, and my son made me happy. I couldn't stay down; I had the unfortunate experience of showing them that a bad relationship is not the end of the world. My son wouldn't leave me alone even when he knew I wanted him to. He's happy, energetic, and hilarious. With all this joy, I knew I needed to keep him busy. Football is his thing, but he's been in basketball, track, soccer, boxing, plumbing class, violin, choir, art, African dance, and drumming. These are a lot of practices to drive to after work. My drive has been to give him the tools he needs to flourish; to show him how to pray, be respectful and where to find confidence and strength. I don't know how many can identify, but I have also put a lot a mental energy into guiding my teenagers into independence. Everything needs balance, and I've tried not to lose myself working and being a mom.

For more than 10yrs, I've been a dancer with Kulu Mele African American Dance & Drum Ensemble and recently the Executive Director. Every year, I wanted to quit. I loved it but was frustrated that I could never properly balance the time to study it like I needed to in order to dance and feel the movements correctly. I gradually learned because I didn't quit. Every time we pulled off a great show, it made me feel like I had magic. Being able to balance all of that getting off work late, making half-crazy dinners, running to football practice, then dance rehearsal in between life…magic!

Recently, it feels like I've been evolving every second. I choose to be happy. I will not let anything or anyone get in the way of that. I won't argue. I choose not to feed into and exchange negative energy back and forth with anyone. I kill people with direct words and kindness. At some point in my stillness, I realized that I need to do a better job setting healthy boundaries with people, including my children for me to have a peaceful life. I believe hard work pays off. I've planted a lot of seeds with family and finances. Sometimes we want things to happen immediately. I'm the type of person that will do four sit-ups, then look in the mirror for results. I, constantly, try to stop my anxiety by having faith. The person that helps me get that together is my older brother, Bro. John Wilkie, minister of Edgewood Church of Christ. When I felt like I was at scratch, I gravitated to him all the way into getting baptized at his church. In our conversations, he made me realize that I was hard on myself. He told me I was "brilliant." I really began to reflect and see my worth differently. I didn't think I was insecure, but I made it intentional to be confident and embrace the gifts God gave me. It's a one day at a time, getting to know your new self-type a thing. To be honest, it's really been easier said than done. I have so much on my plate, that I have a hard time scheduling everything. I decided to put energy into catering to what makes my heart smile. One major thing that makes my heart smile, is to make other people's heart smile…and making money! There are so many people hurting, sad and lost. I'm sure I will continue to figure out how to keep myself productive. Try to remember that you are not in control of the outcome. You give that to the Most High. Every day, push yourself to be a role model for your children. Life is not easy, but if you choose to live, live.

About Fasina Wilkie

Fasina Wilkie grew up in North Philadelphia, the daughter of loving parents deeply involved in the African Drum and Dance Ensemble, Kulu Melé. She is a graduate of Temple University, a Federal Government employee, a divorcee, an African Dancer, and a single mother. She has been to hell and back and has lived to tell her story with the blessing of God. She is hilariously funny, yet shy and sometimes unsure of herself. She is strong willed and loyal to a fault, many times putting the needs of others ahead of her own. She is re-learning who Fasina is while simultaneously leading her children to independence. Fighting institutional racism, traveling whenever and wherever she can, while being both Mom and Dad has not been easy. But with a sip of wine and faith in her heart, she fights on!!! Momming and Queening is Fasina's first anthology. You can follow Fasina at @wildseedwilk_writes on IG and at wildseedwilk_writes on Facebook.

Sad Mama

By JoLynn Bitler

Excerpt from author's journal

I never wanted to be a single mom. In truth, I had a hard time in and of itself being a present, pleasant, purposeful, playful, "good" mom in the first place with my older two children as a married woman. Let alone being in my 40's with my third child, alone without his father. I found myself not only grieving my youngest son's father's death but the death of what I thought my life was going to be. After Jimmy's death, it did not take me long to project my fear and loneliness, anxiety and dread into the future me. I knew I needed safety. Not just for the part of me drowning in my current sorrow with all her overwhelmingly dark feelings but for the future me that I envisioned without Jim.

When my Jim died, my heart broke and my spirit lost all her breath. My dear friend brought me a beautiful water colored poster with a couple of suggestions for self-care that she used to help herself. She said to me with her big, radiant smile, "Here Jo, I brought you this to help you have a happier depression." For whatever reason that struck with me, and I laughed and from then on, I did start to have a happier depression. What struck me about the list on her poster was that it was a list of things I needed to do. It took some semblance of action from me. What it did not say was how long

I was supposed to do it and when and that I had to do it with a smile and that I had to like doing it. It presented hope that if I attempted to try, I believe that it was a promise that the Lord would meet me there. There was hope that I would make progress more away from the sadness and more towards something and maybe toward someone like Himself. I could not see back then that the list was puzzle pieces to a larger canvas. I am grateful for the love of that friend to bring that to me. It was like she was gently, lovingly, without shame placing me on a life raft and pushing me toward safety.

Suggestions to have a Happier Depression.

Sadness can distort the truth and makes it harder to see yourself and the situation clearly. Sadness turns up the voice of the adversary, and it can feel like a part of you died. The Lord can feel far away, and it does make your spiritual life hazy and clouding. Just know that scripture tell us that he will never forsake us. You will feel again. You will see Him. He will make himself known to you. Even those that do not choose him, he still gives grace too. So, my dear heart even if after you attempt some of these suggestions, and it still feels like it leaves you wanting. Do them again. And again. Sometimes sadness cannot feel anything else but itself. Sadness is designed to focus on you and solely on you and what you are not. As a mama, we need other mamas to lift us up. As a sad, grieving mother we need other mamas to lift us up in prayer and comfort. The following points just may help start the process of having a happier depression…

1) **Please get a Bible of your choosing. As well as a journal with lines and a devotional.** On stronger days: Start with dating the page, use the header "Dear Jesus", look up the scripture given to you in Sarah Young's devotional *Jesus Calling.* Copy the scripture and place your name in scripture. This will help you understand scripture was made for you. Underline parts of the devotional that speak to you the

most. Write out your prayers like you are writing a letter to God. As the Spirit leads, he will interweave the devotional in your letter. On those days when your spirit is weak: Take it all with you under the covers, read the scripture allowed and end your prayer saying out loud "Jesus". You have done something far more powerful than you imagine just saying his name out loud.

2) **Approach your sadness gently.** Regard your un-regarded sadness. Un-regarded sadness manifests in anger. Anger that has no resolve turns into depression. Ask for what you need.

3) **Sadness and depression can immobilize you.** You can shut down and shut out the world. Do what is helpful. The key phrase is to do. Opposite action. If you do not feel like showering, it might be helpful to shower. Move at a turtle's pace to get there. Stay in there and cry yourself through it if need be.

4) **Reframe from shaming yourself and please do not accept other's shaming of you.** Shame is most likely the conduit of sadness. Challenge the shame language please remove "should" and "have to" from your list of phrases that use guilt as a motivator.

5) **Please reframe from making the gratitude list.** It just shames you and dismisses you where you are. The gratitude list usually screams that you have no right to be sad because look at all God has done for you. The Lord does not use what he gives you to shame you. Instead make a list of who God is and who He is to you.

6) **Sadness can make you physically hurt, and it lowers your immune system.** Sadness can show up through pain. Please see your physician. The very least go to urgent

care. Physicians have list of referral sources such as counselor as well.

7) **Play.** As a sad, depressed or grieving mama person, we can forget our purpose, and we forget we can play. Sometimes we are not just sad about the past, but we can be overwhelmingly sad about the present. We need to surround ourselves with friends and playful children. Go down a slide mommy, splash in puddles, kick a ball around, play hide and go seek. Find that playful child part of you and connect with your children.

8) **Purpose.** We have a purpose here. We are so busy growing up little adults, we cannot see past that the little creatures are amazing and have intricate parts to them that is beyond just being a part of you. Cultivate that part of you again; that is intricately you. God created you in his image. What parts of God are in you that make you feel special? We all need to feel special. We all need to feel seen. Sometimes we need to search for that part of us or reawaken it.

9) **Half Smile.** It is a compromise. Instead of smiling and instead of frowning- half smile. It is different when you half smile when you are angry; that is passive aggression. Half smile is like a way you are silently fighting your inner battle. You are not acting like you are not, but you are not giving into it either.

10) **Take a walk, sleep and drink water.** When we are sad, depressed or grieving we forget the things that ground us to the present, that are helpful to our bodies. Exercise, sleep and the right foods nourish us and help our immune systems and decrease stress hormones and aide our nervous system. Research in mood disorders especially Bipolar show that the main ingredients to managing mood is to balance out these three.

11) **2 Corinthians 10:5.** Take every thought captive. Challenge your thoughts. Challenge your belief system about yourself and about God. We have automatic thoughts that come. Although we are not guilty of having intrusive thoughts that we do not mean to have; we are responsible for how we respond to them. Intrusive thoughts act like a bully reminding you of your fears and secrets; threatening you. These are not of God. Yet, you can use these thoughts to surrender to Him. A good clinician who has training in Cognitive Behavior Therapy and or Obsessive-Compulsive Disorder along with a solid foundation of biblical doctrine can help separate between the lies and the Truth.

12) **Prevention.** Maybe we will use the word "Acceptance" in place of prevention. When we have our good days, we don't ever want to feel unhappiness "like that" again. We can fear ever being in the dark place of sadness, depression, grief, loneliness and despair. However, it can happen, and we can ease the fear of it by accepting it will happen. Write a letter from your happy part to your sad part. Reminding the sad part that you will overcome and that you will not stay in the dark for long. Write a letter reminding the sad part what she needs to do for herself when she is sad. Encourage her to keep taking small steps forward.

13) **Relapse Plan.** A relapse plan is an intentional plan of action to implement when you have found yourself in a sad, depressed, grieving cycle again. We can forget that some of us are vulnerable to the seasons changing. We can be exceptionally more susceptible to depression around anniversary dates of events that can trigger a depression cycle such as divorce, dates, or anniversary of a loved one's death. Our bodies can remember pain.

14) **Be mindful of unhelpful dissociations.** Dissociations do not have to be as extreme as having an out of body experience. It can be subtle such as driving a car and realizing you were not mindful of the road because you were lost in thought. Dissociations like these can be dangerous. Be careful not to use substances to dissociate for too long, then it becomes an addiction and much higher consequences. Rather distractions such as reading (preferably something uplifting), binge watching a Netflix series (nothing sad) or listening to music (nothing nostalgic from your teenage years) maybe helpful.

15) **Reach out to someone else.** Reach out to a trusted girl-friend. When we are sad, depressed and grieving we want to isolate and seclude ourselves. Reach out and let some-one you trust know what is going on or at least pray for you or with you. Text your friends a "Checking In" text. It is helpful to know that it is not all about us at times.

16) **Most of us sad, depressed and grieving mama's wish we could hide under the covers.** If only. We push ourselves to keep busy and to keep going because we have little people to take care of. We push ourselves, but we do not regard ourselves. Mothers are doers. We focus on doing rather than what we are being. We may be displaying a defense against feeling sad, depressed, grieving or anxious or angry. We are not in the present when we drive ourselves to do. We are not actually accepting or dealing with what is; we are moving to get things done. The more we create the less vulnerable we feel. Doing is a way to avoid, and yet, we are being this example to our children.

17) **Do no harm.** Sadness, depression and grief can harm others just as it harms you. Learn to express, examine and work toward a resolution. Without a resolution your feelings

can spill over to others and directly or unintentionally hurt your loved ones.

18) **Hang on, hope is here in the present.** Jeremiah 29:11. "For I know the plans I have for you," declares the Lord; "plans to give you hope and a future." Yes, the Lord will provide for us in the future. We can make a list of what he has provided, and we know despite how we feel that we will get through the hole we are in. When we are in the sad, depressed, grieving hole, we have an opportunity. Read Jeremiah 29: 12-14. "Then you will call upon me and come to pray to me and I will listen to you. You will seek me and find me when you seek me with all your heart." He knew we would be in the hole and in need of Him. He gives us two promises not only does he have plans for us in future, but we have the promise of Him in the now.

Regardless of how we became sad, depressed or how we came to grief or what trauma we have walked out of -or currently walking in, we all have a story to tell. As a single mother, an alienated mother, a grieving mom, a mom who is married yet walking alone emotionally neglected by her partner. Regardless our story can be one of triumph. As I write this, I am not only a single mom, but thriving professional who has walked alongside listening to many of mother's stories. Learning as I go to be a student; learning to hold on to their stories without judgment. To be a witness of their resilience. As a Christian woman who was given wisdom during my pain. Make my journey purposeful. As I go through my episodes of depression, I also come out with one more piece of the puzzle. One more aspect that will help me get through the next and the next. We are not promised a painless life, but we are promised that when we seek Him through it with all our hearts, He will be found by us.

About JoLynn Bitler

JoLynn Bitler is a Licensed Professional Mental Health Counselor currently practicing in the state of Delaware. She graduated with a bachelor's in Human Services and went on to obtain her Master's degree in Marriage and Family Therapy. In addition, she is also a National Credentialed Counselor in the United States. Professionally, she has a history of working with a plethora of people with different backgrounds and concerns. JoLynn boasts about how much she loves what she does. She is in awe and inspired every day, by the people who honor her by allowing her to walk with them through life's trials. Her professional life is accented by her personal journey through being a solo mother, an independent woman, a practitioner, an inspiring author, a grieving (yet healing) heart and person that professes to be completely dependent on her relationship with Jesus Christ. JoLynn enjoys swimming, her children, reading, music and movies and adventure and facing down her fears. You can connect with JoLynn through her Facebook page, "Rooted in Grace Therapy." If interested and the need arises, you can reach "Jo" through her practice at jolynnbitler@rootedingracetherapy.com.

It's What you Make It

By Alesha Shaw

Parenting in today's age is, let me just say, is different. I am learning that it is one of those things that you just have to make your own. You use family values and customs as guides, but at the end of the day, you have to tailor it to fit the needs of your children and family. I think that is where we go wrong sometimes; trying to fit in the mold that someone else created.

No one really knows what to expect when they become mothers. They have ideas of the type of mom they would be and what they will and will not do. Some of us have even been guilty of judging other's mothering, as if we can do a better job or have a better solution. Side note: one thing that irks my soul is projecting what you would do on to what someone should do. Truth of the matter is, once that baby pops out, it's like having a blank piece of paper in front of you and having no idea what to write. Sure, the experience is beautiful (somewhat, because Lawd knows, my kids took everything out of me), but the reality is, life changes in a way that we are sometimes not ready for.

When I had my oldest daughter nine years ago, I was happy to be a mother. I never doubted that I wouldn't be able to take care of her. I wasn't worried or concerned about much at all, at first. My only disappointment was that I wouldn't have a tribe around me to help. I am all the way in Delaware, and my family lives in the south, Texas and Louisiana. My in-laws were also in Texas and the rest of my husband's family lives on the island of Jamaica. Thankfully, my mother-in-law came to live with us for the first 3 months of my daughter's life and helped tremendously. When she left, I was confident I would be ok, and for the most part I was.

Naturally, I just took on motherhood with no hesitation, and not putting much thought into it. Everywhere I went, she went. Although, my husband could have kept her, I always planned to take her anywhere I planned to go that my husband wasn't going to go. If I was shopping, she was there. Going to a pageant, she was there. Going to a "send-off" party, she was there. Work, she was there (sometimes). I brought her with no hesitation. It wasn't until I had my second daughter, and my oldest was getting older, that I thought, wait a minute! This is getting kind of tough.

After my youngest, things started to shift in me. It became more difficult to share myself. I was being spread too thin. It seemed everyone needed me. Literally 3 weeks after I had my second daughter, my oldest won her first pageant. So, right away, I was involved in pageant activities and making sure she met her responsibilities. All while nursing a newborn and settling into becoming a mommy of 2. I was always on the go and was barely finding time to dress myself. There were definitely times I left the house, and my appearance was very "motherly," no style whatsoever. Then, there was my husband who also needed my attention. It was a lot. I found myself thinking. I only have 2 kids, how in the world do mothers of more than 2 handle it. I quickly changed my desire to have 3 kids to, yeah, I'm done!! I went into survival mode. I, honestly, do know how I did it, but

I was taking care of everyone's needs not realizing I wasn't taking care of my own.

It was at the beginning of 2020, my daughters, 2 and 7, that I started to feel like something had to give. I was just existing. Everything just felt automatic. I was going about each day a shell of a person. There but not really there. I was miserable at work. Feeling overlooked, mistreated, and taken advantage of. Drained by motherhood and wifey-hood. I wasn't doing anything for myself. Self-care? Where? So, when we were told we were on lockdown, I silently, said, "Thank you, Jesus!" I needed things to slow down so I could gather myself.

So, as COVID-19 hit, and we all sat, shut in our homes. I decided to utilize this time to really focus on my spiritual growth and my growth as a mother. I had become irritated with my children, and my patience was running thin. I lost interest in things that used to excite me. I would feel like crying for no reason, and always felt tired and irritable. It was like a dark cloud constantly hovering over me, and I couldn't shake it. I found myself constantly complaining and having desires to do better and to work on goals I set, but never having the energy to even pursue or start them. I felt I was failing in the motherhood department. I realized I needed to retreat and make time for me so that I can fill my cup. That's it! I was trying to pour from an empty cup.

I started journaling and reading the bible. I was doing some serious praying and trying to connect with God, asking Him some hard and honest questions. I needed to know what was going on with me so that I can be a better, present mother. Not present physically, but mentally, and not just an empty shell. I started seeing that I was holding myself to this standard of motherhood that I, myself, couldn't reach. I had in my head the idea of what a mother is and what she should be doing. And get this, that vision didn't even fit my personality, I was setting an unrealistic goal for myself. For instance, I don't like cooking. That skill skipped me. I have great cooks in my family, and for some reason, I must have been doing something I had no business doing when God was giving out the gift of cooking because he skipped over me. Knowing this, why was I putting pressure on myself to be that cook? Then, I would feel bad when I couldn't achieve this and would draw the conclusion that because I lack, I am not good enough. However, I had to learn that the little meals that I can cook are sufficient for them. Besides my youngest will alternate eating mac 'n' cheese and rice every day and will be content!!

Then, there was this whole monitoring of these new age devices (phones, tablets, iPads, laptop). When I was growing up, we had to make sure movies weren't rated 'R' and mostly kept the TV on Nickelodeon. Now, they have the world in the palm of their hands. Anybody can create a YouTube channel and create content. Many times, the "kids" look young, so you assume the content is ok, but after listening, you realize, not all parents filter their children's speech and are ok with their children speaking any kind of way. To each his own, but not in my house. No matter how many parental controls I put on, things are bound to get through exposing them to something I don't want them to be exposed. What is worse, they know more about technology than I do. I started to get overwhelmed with always monitoring what other people were putting out. Worrying that my child will surely lose her innocence if I cannot shelter her from the things of the world. It is too much; I just cannot do it all. I started to say, "Alesha, just teach them what is right and what you expect. Trust that they will know what is right and wrong. Guess what? Any time a person says something inappropriate, my oldest switches the video.

You know what else had me tripping? Those things that were instilled in us from generation to generation. There are a lot of sayings and ideas that are projected on to us, giving us the notion that this is how we are to parent. These things don't even fit my parenting style or personality, but I felt I had to follow because hey, that was my blueprint. For example, I allow my oldest daughter to express herself. Meaning, if she is feeling some type of way about something, I let her express it. Now, if she is out of line, she will definitely be corrected, but I want her to feel like she has a voice, and I want her to feel safe expressing things to me. However, traditionally, that hasn't been accepted. You do what you are told, and you don't have a say-so. If a parent (adult figure) makes a mistake, it is what it is, and you don't say anything. If I make a mistake, I apologize. If she is feeling upset or sad, I let her tell me why. However, I started to question if this was the right thing to do. Am I being her "friend" or am I being her parent? Am I killing her spirit if I limit her expression? Would others mistake this as a lack of parenting? The pressure I put on myself was tremendous, and all it did was made me feel like a failure. I kept feeling like I was coming up short.

After praying and asking God for wisdom and under-standing and trying to figure out what was wrong with me, what was revealed to me was that I needed to relax. He clearly said, "Girl, you need to chill. There is nothing wrong with you." Sure, there are times where I am exhausted and overwhelmed from trying to protect them and make sure they know right from wrong. Times where I feel like I am losing my mind because I swear, I have repeated myself more than I can count. Times where I told them to get off YouTube, yet I hear another video start. Times that the role of mommy is just not my thing. Let's be real, some days I just don't want to mommy. But I remember that He says, *"Come to me, all you who are weary and burdened, and I will give you rest. Take my yoke upon you and learn from me, for I am gentle and humble in heart, and you will find rest for your souls. For my yoke is easy and my burden is light."* ~Matthew 11:28-30. Being overwhelmed comes with the territory but that doesn't make me a bad mother, nor does it mean something is wrong with me. Sure, I don't always have the answers, and maybe some days I am missing the mark, but there are also those days that I am doing the dang thing.

I say to you. Motherhood is what you make it. You choose how you want to mother your children. All that matters is that you have done the best you can, and they know at the end of the day, you have their best interest at heart. You don't have to follow traditions or anything else that was instilled in you. Create your own thing. You are the Queen of your castle. YOU have the power to set the atmosphere of your family. Lastly, it is nobody's business what you do and how run your household, so stop worrying about what others are doing and thinking because we are all in the same boat.

So, with my girls, sometimes we TikTok, some days we dance around in the kitchen to Beyonce', other days I am screaming at the top of my lungs for my oldest to clean up her mess for the umpteen time, and telling the little one, "No, I'm not interested in sitting in the bathroom while you poop!" But whatever day it is, I'm going to always mom it and queen it!! And I am sure you are doing the same!!

To the Ladies of the Momming and Queening Anthology

I just want to say "THANK YOU" for believing in my vision of Momming and Queening. It means so much to me that you ladies trusted me with your stories and were brave enough to share them with others. You are true examples of what I wanted this book to be about. Women who were showing the magic of motherhood despite challenges. I am sure your stories will touch someone, and I pray that you enjoyed this journey as much as I did. Please know you are rocking this thing. Wear that crown proudly as you continue to mom it and queen it!!

"Her children rise up and call her blessed; her husband also, and he praises her: 'Many women have done excellently, but you surpass them all.'" ~Proverbs 31:28–29

Made in the USA
Middletown, DE
09 August 2021

45717372R00046